DARWIN'S CIRCUS

Poems by
Edward Fisher

Order this book online at www.trafford.com
or email orders@trafford.com

Most Trafford titles are also available at major online book retailers.

Printed in the United States of America.

ISBN: 978-1-4669-2050-7 (sc)
ISBN: 978-1-4669-2049-1 (e)

Trafford rev. 03/29/2012

 www.trafford.com

North America & international
toll-free: 1 888 232 4444 (USA & Canada)
phone: 250 383 6864 ♦ fax: 812 355 4082

CONTENTS

ADAGIO TO LIGHT 1

Like You...3
The Orchard East in Light 4
X, Stick-Figure 5
Sunday 7
Fine-Feathered Hearts 10
Atonement 11
The Hollow Body of God..12
Before the Writers of the Bible...13
The Human Face..15
If I Could Send a Grief to God 16
The Darkside of God...18
The Secret of Joy 19
Death Kept Its Promise...20
Beginning All Over..21

THE DAYS GO DANCING ROUND THE POLES 23

The Hinge of Morning...25
Xylem & Phloem..27
Dew on the Insect Dynamo 29
The Synthesis Of Light..31
Eight Wild Birds Looking for Food.....................................32
Bye-Bye Cocoon.. 34
Jazzamataz 36
Deja Vu..38
Darwin's Circus 40
Animal Alphabets 41
The Spirit of Stallions...42

Arc of the Moon..43
Compost 45
Cloud Atlas 46
Lord of the Magic Hammer 48
Arcadian Graces...49
The Residue of Day 51
Loose Leaf...52
Rainspouts Are All Icy 54
Soft Snow Slow Sinking.....................................56
Perfect Snow 57
Above the Tree-Line..58
Zygote...59
The Days Go Dancing Round the Poles 60

LOVE'S COMPASS ROSE 63

Sleep Lay Long...65
Roughly, Softly 66
The Land Where Love Lies Down.......................67
Wonderful Indigo Tapestry................................68
Land of the Lost and Found...............................69
Heart of Dove & Wing of Sparrow 70
Walk Softly in My Garden..................................71
There Were Birds in the Room this Morning 72
Hushed Hosannas..73
With Poetry on my Lips.....................................74
Heloise & Abelard...75
Pressed Petals 77
Love Song 78
Coordinates...80
Time's Voices Speak Through Me 81
O, The Perfect Poetic..82

ACKNOWLEDGEMENTS

Grateful acknowledgement is due the editors and publishers of a number of publications in which the following poems first appeared:

Advocate: "Bye Bye Cocoon", "Déjà vu"; *The Alembic:* "Days Go Dancing Round the Poles"; *Art Times:* "Coordinates"; *Avocet:* "Arcadian Graces"; *Crucible:* "Sunday"; *Dream Fantasy International* "Zygote"; *FreeXpression*: "Atonement", "The Orchard East in Light"; *The Griffin*: "Land of the Lost & Found"; *Hidden Oak* "Compost"; *Ibbetson St. Press:* "Xylem & Phloem"; *Illuminations*: "Hinge of the Morning"; *Jones Av:* "Rainspouts Are All Icy"; *The Journal:* "Land Where Love Lies Down", "Death Kept Its Promise"; *Love's Chance* "Roughly / Softly"; *The Lyric:* "Synthesis of Light"; *Mr. Marquis Museletter:* "Soft Snow, Slow Sinking"; *Pegasus:* "Love Song"; *Penwood Review*: "The Hollow Body of God"; *Plainsongs:* "Hushed Hosannas"; *The Poet's Art:* "Time's Voices Speak through Me", "Beginning All Over"; *Poet's Pen:* "X, Stick-Figure", "If I Could Send a Grief to God"; *Poetry Motel / Chronogram:* "Sleep Lay Long"; *Poetsespresso:* "Eight Wild Birds Looking for Food"; *Quantum Leap:* "The Residue of Day", Dew on the Insect Dynamo", "There Were Birds in the Room This Morning": *Quercus Review & Plain Spoke*: "Jazzamataz"; *Science Editor:* "Darwin's Circus"; *The Shepard*: "Like You"; *Straylight:* "Heart of Dove & Wing of Sparrow"; *Tale Spinners:* "Pressed Petals"; *Taproot:* "The Human Face"; *The Taylor Trust:* "Wonderful Indigo Tapestry", "The Secret of Joy"; *Texas Wesleyan University:* "Atonement"; *Write On!!:* "Spirit of Stallions"; *The Writer & Sanskrit:* "O, the Perfect Poetic"; *Writers' Journal* "Fine-Feathered Hearts".

To Gayle, Sabriya & Gowon

"Eternity is in love with the productions of time . . ."

~William Blake

ADAGIO TO LIGHT

LiKE YOU

Like you I like a festive hunt for eggs—
I like to come upon them in the grass
Where crickets rub their legs and drink the dew,
Surprised by rabbits hieing in the spring!
I like to wake up early when the birds
Build silhouetted wings against the sky . . .
I feel a deeper, secret sorrow then
Than any other time. Not in a church
Nor rapt and ragged place beyond the soul,
But through a simple pane of glass observe
The ritual renewals of rebirth,
The sacrifice and mystery of the cross.
The colors and the glory are all there
When sunlight parts with shadow on the earth.

Edward Fisher

THE ORCHARD EAST IN LIGHT

The orchard east in light, an ancient orange,
Pours through the stain-glass precincts of the dawn;
Creaks open like an old cathedral door-hinge
Where hymns are hushed and nesting songbirds yawn—
Atlantis at my window, pigeon-holed;
Nirvana's lotus-blossom breathlessness;
The Garden gone to seed, an Age of Gold
That borders on Elysium's lost address!

Eternity retells its haunting story
As curving earth renews an age-old grief;
Cloud-bound resorts and uncaged zoos of glory
In tapestry of time and turning leaf . . .
Each breath, a flower exhaled, a dream that fades,
Where beasts lie down together in the shade.

4

X, STICK-FIGURE

I am the sky.
I am the root
And the ring
Of the tree.
I am the sea;
Hands of the children
Teaching the beasts
Humility.

I am the word.
I am the blood
And the truth
On the wing.
Unto the heart
In the traffic
And throng,
I am the reckoning.

I am the bread.
I am the voice
And the face
In the wine.
I am the dead;
Birds that have fallen,
Loves that are lost
Are mine.

I am the lamb.
Palms of the hands
Sign of the man
That shall be.
Vision of tenderness,
Wisdom and psalm;
Iambic feet
On the sea.

SUNDAY

This One
From whom
All faces turn
All flowers yearn
All fires burn
The Sun

Emerging like an egg
On the space of this page
And the day where I move
With love, through my rooms
In this memoir of mornings—

Lying awake
On clean white sheets
With dew on the lawn,
My mother's voice
Lost in a song
Downstairs in the kitchen;
Her dishwater hands
Threading a needle,
Shrinking the world
To the soles of my feet;
Sewing my shadow back on . . .

What wonderful dark little swallows!
What beautiful sky-blue ovals!
What pigeon-holes! What views!
So round, so full of sighs and whispers . . .

And me & my sisters
All dressed up in our Sunday best,
With dad on the couch
In his glory, snoring
Under the Sunday papers,
On this, his one day of rest . . .

Like organ-pipes
Soaring, in chorus,
In the hush & shuffle of feet
As the congregation
Takes their seats . . .

Myself by the altar
In acolyte's robes,
Lighting the candles,
Humming the hymnals
In the little brick church
Just down the road
From the drive-in movie,
Where I sinned on a dare,
And stole my first kiss,
Played class-clown for laughs
And fought with my fists;
Caught a copperhead snake,
Ate bacon & grits . . .
And earned my God & Country,
Hoping to escape
By the skin of my teeth
The Beast in the underground silo . . .

The voice of Caruso
Lost in the *Lord's Prayer,*
Awake in my cot
By the lake, after taps . . .

At peace in this place at last,
This echoing hollow
Full of hellos and good-byes

Darkening bird's wing
Beckoning O
Becoming all hallow

FINE-FEATHERED HEARTS

Bring back all persons, cursed, disowned;
All hidden halves, all dark sides shown;
Whatever was unloved make whole;
Bid welcome to your soul.

What guest among us so despised
Is not some child by time disguised?
These hands and feet make free to move;
Come take your stand in love!

The marble moon was once a bust:
Estranged, its faces come to dust;
All disembodied thoughts embrace
The noble brow made base.

These things that we cut off from us
Make up one world—what always was;
These tear-stained pages, years alone,
Beauty disdained, unknown.

All the unwanted of the earth,
Gone their belongings, of no worth,
Back to the land of the lost and found
Long ago shadows underground.

Fine-feathered hearts that flee from me,
That break like waves, beat wings to sea—
Let light be rhymed with night, one poem;
Make of my hearth one home.

ATONEMENT

However deep the sun is sinking
   Into dreams,
Color me a rainbow,
Paint longing on my soul . . .

Whosever face the moon is hiding
   In the sea,
Divided waters of my heart
Break like the waves in shells.

Wherever psalms are sung at evening
   Take me home
Till rivers reach my mouth
And journeys are no more . . .

Whenever time to idle nothing
   Whiles away,
Let every valley have a voice
And every joy a flower.

Whatever way the world is spinning
   Let me go
And stand out on the edge,
My shadow left behind . . .

Forever as the stars are falling
   Lay me down:
My body one with life on earth;
My open eyes, the sky.

THE HOLLOW BODY OF GOD

Be still as a pool of water after rain,
Free & light as the song of morning birds,
Quiet as a dewdrop disappearing, or
A millennium of stone undisturbed . . .

Be tranquil as the shade of an old oak,
Easy as a dog by a rocking chair,
Mild as a gentle breeze rustling the leaves,
Calm as evening's hush under the eaves.

Be soothing as a mother's lullaby,
Serene as whispering lovers abed
And motionless as the unrotating moon
Speaking from the hollow body of God . . .

Whose footstool is wisdom full of pity,
Whose heart is a dark, floating mountain,
Whose ancient elephant caryatid
Holds up the dream-world of your sleeping head.

BEFORE THE WRITERS OF THE BIBLE

Before the Bible there was the Word beyond words
Written into the elemental fine-print of the night,
Endlessly repeated on the inky pages of nothingness.

Before hieroglyphs were chiseled into the pyramids,
Before the builders of Babel & the Ten Antediluvian Kings,
Before diligent men transcribed histories on crumbling papyrus . . .

A play of shadows, a dream-time record, a Book of the Dead,
Discovered in the dry salt of an ancient desert riverbed
Shedding its skin under the changing pageantry of the moon!

Before the hero conquered Leviathan & the dragon was slain,
The snake in the garden was a god in his own right,
Master of rebirth, revered for seven millennium . . .

Alias Ramses & Moses, Adonis & Jesus, Osiris & Zeus,
The myth of the blind king waxes, the fable of the lame king wanes—
Echoes of the resurrection redeemed on the tips of pagan tongues!

Before the Fall in Eden, the planet itself fell endlessly around the sun—
The parting of the waters is the crowning of the universal womb;
Woman come from a cage of bone; man from a bloody wound.

The legends of exile, the tales of fire & flood,
The graven image & the revelation on the mountain
Are age-old stories rewritten by each new generation . . .

A pinch of divinity is immanent in every sand-grain & raindrop;
The eternal wonders of the World-Knot
And the convolutions of the brain are one & the same.

Fossil imprints on drifting continents cry out in substratum layers of
      rock:
"God-in-man's-image is the kindergarten of the soul!"
"The Bible is our nursery rhyme, a playroom full of children's toys!"

Hallucinations & daydreams govern our waking imaginations—
Pompous deceivers & pious believers dictate divine design,
Concocting Apocryphal phantoms & intoxicating hypocrisies!"

We are called upon to marvel at the spinning demons in the atom
And the awesome spectacle of a billion whirling galaxies!
The earth is a secret seed in search of a silent scripture . . .

We are witness to the mystery, at the threshold to the labyrinth,
Held hostage to a monstrous cosmic drama,
The tragedy of time revealed & concealed every moment.

Mercy is a higher kind of truth; laughter like bread & wine.
Destiny is whimsical; even God surprises himself,
But only widows & orphans know how to sing . . .

THE HUMAN FACE

In every face I see the halo of a fallen saint:
A hidden journey through a valley of grief & despair
Where witness is written in the fabric of knitted brows—
The threads of wisdom from which the universe is woven.

In every smile, the thin veneer of civilization
Curves around sensuous lips to a twisted, angry mouth;
Agony vanishes into old familiar wounds
And the bruised asylum of infinite sun-split clouds.

In every mirror, the vision of a murdered god
Wrinkled over the soft, kissed, daydreaming cheek of childhood;
In the pupil of every eye, the inexhaustible
Mystery of laughter confronting burnt cities & barbed wire.

Every hair, a fine distinction between sorrow & glory,
Half spiritual experiment, half heaven's ambition;
Cries of joy are on the tongue of every holy hunger
And a silent hymn uncurling in every stranger's ear!

IF I COULD SEND A GRIEF TO GOD

If I could send a grief to God,
A wing to mend, wrapt in a leaf;
Heart-broken halves, unspoken fears,
The cares that waste away the years . . .

From nowhere in the upper air
Trespassers of the light escape
Beyond all words, death's whispered shape,
Held breaths go mouthing cloud-bound prayers—

The shadow of some hidden hand
Makes motherless this no-man's land;
Corrupts the world with shameless lies,
Gives homelessness its nameless eyes,

And wages genocidal war
Against the innocent and the poor;
The lonely, scorned and orphaned child—
Life without hope, debased, defiled.

Our destiny made manifest:
The gentle races dispossessed,
And self-destruction's marketplace
Lends suffering a human face.

Be it forever here resolved:
Return with mercy, work and love,
And justice in the bargain prove;
Let us yet learn how to forgive!

If I could send a grief to God:
Psalm on the wind, beyond a yawn;
Dawn in the garden gone to seed,
Last song of lost love wished upon . . .

Below my lattice spills the moon,
Shadowy strangers fill my room;
To fall so far, so fast asleep
Without a star, so dark, so deep . . .

God sends me sights and sounds by day
And dreams by night to light my way
Through darkness, while the whole world sleeps;
I pray Godspeed and keep you safe.

THE DARKSIDE OF GOD

No one has chronicled the courage, as yet,
Of those for whom no miracle cures were found; who
Wake up every morning, get out of bed
And mount that heroic struggle, just to do
What we all take for granted, file & forget,
Like buttoning a shirt, or lacing up a shoe . . .

On the road through ashes & despair to love
We encounter a wheelchair, a crutch & a riddle,
And shudder at the utter fragility of life.
Suffering makes an opening for the soul
Where the shadow of laughter passes through grief—
A hurt that becomes our gift to the world . . .

The mind's divided mirror cuts us off—
The crippled child, the homeless & the odd
Are our spiritual twins, the other half
Of a secret genius we keep well-hid;
Our wounded nakedness, our orphaned self;
The undiscovered, darker side of God.

The task before us: to grow a new heart
Like old-growth oak a lightning-bolt has sundered,
And, climbing down into the depths of that scar,
Stand up, breathe in & learn to walk all over!
To rediscover who we really are
And were born to be: *helpless without each other . . .*

THE SECRET OF JOY
(for Sabriya)

"What is the secret of joy?" You ask—
Wind rippling over water slowly.
Hold tight to all the pieces; attend the light.
This is your only consolation.

Take all the discarded postcards
And love-letters of your heart,
Every sigh & smiling remembrance,
And decide on a new arrangement . . .

After the hardness of winter
Let the icicle follow its whim
Into the raindrops of spring.
There is no right or wrong way.

Let your middle be your end;
Let your end be your beginning—
Peace of mind is all.

Gather everything in your arms
And throw it into the sky
Like autumn leaves . . .

Lift up, cast aside & try again.
Dying is not a bad thing,
Only a new chance to play.

Edward Fisher

DEATH KEPT ITS PROMISE

Death kept its promise,
Kindly did it come;
Pain before forbearance
Struggled into seed.

Dolorous, marvelous
Earth whose ear
Has grown incredibly deaf,
Heed these words.

Listening light,
Whispering waves,
Moisten these lips
With the kiss of leaves.

Blossom and burn:
Fires, flowers.

BEGINNING ALL OVER

He is simply beginning all over,
Rushing headlong towards the world;
Becoming what he always was
And will always be,
Only this time the search will be richer.

His joy will make a difference now because
He had the privilege and the courage
To return to his own sources
Under new and hopeful voices
And helping hands.

And he will be remade in a way that he always is
Every minute,
Only this time under subtle tutelage
And with simpler graces,
The image of himself in freer form

Kicking his way into light and laughter!
He is simply beginning all over,
Slipping again from this world of our arms
And into the next,
As we try to hold him back.

THE DAYS
GO DANCING
ROUND THE POLES

THE HINGE OF MORNING

Anonymous earth
Aches on its axis
Oiling the tiny bones of the ear
Creaking off key like an old rusty hinge . . .

And so it begins:
This secret circuit of inner connections
Calling my name,
Unlocking the tumblers of morning.

Part mimic, part heartbreak,
Part tympanic membrane
Eavesdropping on glory,
Fine-tuning a breath on the wing . . .

An encore to autumn
Applauding like leaves on the far side of dreams,
Seeking to serve as a perch
For my song.

Echoing swallows throat in their turn
Threading the light of day,
Tightening the tap
Like a leaky faucet.

A porch door ajar slams shut!
Sap from a stop
Dripping its liquid note in a pail
Leaves a hole in the sky.

Completing the circle,
Sleep-angled elbow & wrist,
Making their slow-motion changes,
Bending toward rhyme.

XYLEM & PHLOEM

I am learning patience from small animals
Who hide in the shadows & stay out of sight,
Moving around by moonlight . . .

I watch from the underside of leaves
As the chameleon changes & begins to blend in
And the gecko quietly scampers to its nook . . .

Like a butterfly, I drink the tears
From the eyes of the great sea tortoise . . .
My heart is beating in the crocodile's mouth!

O beautiful consciousness lurking around every corner,
I too am listening, holding my breath,
Waiting at the threshold of a lost world!

Dumb luck has brought us here against all odds,
Out of the virtuoso music of xylem & phloem,
The immemorial lottery of minnow & ovum . . .

Our cells are like quicksilver coursers
Running rings around the prehistoric past,
Embracing a new, more joyful self!

We belong here as much as any place else
Like fossils of seashell found in the desert
Containing the memory of everywhere!

Sh-sh-sh! Be still & listen . . .
Our epitaphs are wafted on the wind,
Blowing through the rafters, creaking in the floorboards . . .

Maybe what a poem is for
Is to bend, like the hinges of a door,
Turning the colors of time inside out.

DEW ON THE INSECT DYNAMO

A factory in the plants
By suction pumps
Its secret mineral oils
Up mighty trunks.

Sun-powered, flower-pedaled
Tiny wheels
Lift syrups up on pulleys
Rainbow-milled.

Hypnotic pollens
Propagate the green,
And moonglow-guided orchestras
Rub elbows with the Queen.

Dew on the insect dynamo
This spring
Comes nectar-driven
Dusting off its wings!

A caterpillar
Bivouacked on a leaf
Emerges from its chrysalis
In light's leitmotif.

Antennae-tapping
Elfin troubadours,
Serenading grass-blades
Tune-up their guitars.

A dancing dream a-buzz—
Brain-waves alive
With micro-energies—
A honey-humming hive

Eavesdropping on Elysium
With compound eyes,
Redeems a strident planet
Sandman-size.

THE SYNTHESIS OF LIGHT

New leaf in-laid with dewdrops, vein & stem,
At dawn begins its synthesis of light;
By day, the play of shadows on the wind
And the oxygen-carbon cycle all night.

From doorstep to horizon, nature's brush
Paints process & perspective, landscape scenes
Soft on a falling planet, in the hush
Of pollen, seeds & palettes daubed with greens.

Old alchemies of gold poured from the sun
Absorbed, stored up in deep, concentric rings;
A pithy scroll, a story told in tongues
That secretly renews all living things . . .

The sibyl, breathing out the parts of speech,
As we breathe in the syllables of sleep.

Edward Fisher

EIGHT WILD BIRDS LOOKING FOR FOOD

      Murmuring starlings
Stirring up dead leaves,
Eddy & flock,
Banking for berries.

Daring the pavements
For morsels of road-kill,
Shadowy mimics—
      A murder of crows.

Swaggering for seeds
At my feeder all winter,
      The cardinal holds court
In his crimson robes.

Hammering his hollow notes
On the still standing dead,
      The woodpecker echoes
Checking for insects . . .

Handsome as a pale blue sky
      The jay returns
Raising a ruckus,
Feasting on acorns.

Tugging at earthworms,
     The red-breasted robin,
Harbinger of spring,
Chirrups & hops on my lawn.

Smallest of all,
Hovering & flying backwards,
     The hummingbird darts
Needling for nectar

     Pigeons in the city
Hunt under a park bench
For breadcrumbs & popcorn
Where the homeless man snores.

BYE-BYE COCOON

With easy ahs and ohs and eyes of awe,
My daughter is a cherub in disguise.
Just twenty months and going on forever,
She feels an affinity for all things small,
Especially the chrysalis bivouacked
By the lattice near the back porch step.

Her mother and she inspect it daily,
Anxious for signs of butterfly or moth,
Expecting some Emperor of Silks
Or caterpillar sporting a bright bow-tie
Emerging *circa* sideshows in a shell
From its antediluvian slumbers.

The crisis, growing slowly, is sure to come:
The tadpole's tail is lost on the toad,
The young fry twisting turns its eye to light;
Old ways cast off, old habits left behind,
Till the self is sloughed, the familiar flesh,
Like a marvelous garment, melts away . . .

The mother ministers to her like a muse
Whispering of the old metamorphosis—
Coiled spring of feelers and wings unfolding
Feeding on syrup and starfish and snow—
Mapping out the mysteries of moonlight
From blueprints of the afterlife of clouds.

Timekeeper of the transmigration
Manufactured over millennium
And circulating like flowers in the blood—
Essence of rainbow-imago in gold
Brewed from ethereal extracts of oils
And the commonplace substance of tears.

The lowly worm knows nothing of magic,
Hears only the tightening cords of the throat,
The lump of all departures swallowed back
As the fluttering heart of the world goes by in a blur
That stirs to utter but cannot cry:
Bye-bye cocoon, bye-bye!

JAZZAMATAZ

1

A seagull circled the jack-straw
Haystack splinter remains
Of a house that stood on a block between
The city and its bypass—
Circled something in the upturned earth
Near a bulldozer tread in the rain . . .

Kept from landing by the angry haw
And ignition of the gruff machine,
It perched atop a telephone pole,
Surveying the scene and the ground beneath
Like prey in a wave as the city extends
Its limits . . .

There are seagulls on the San Francisco bay
Picturesque among popcorn and graffiti . . .

2

Farewell clings to my homesick lips
Like a double-bass riff
At the street-corner junction to nowhere;
Headline extras litter the news—
Dreams down-the-drain,
Round-trip to the sticks, at rush-hour!
All aboard for the blues—

3
Saxophones blow bubbles over seacoast towns
New York to New Orleans,
Where cockroaches crawl through the Greyhound lounge,
And the sky is a single concrete gray,
And the tug in the bay is a ten ton sound!

Saxophone pelicans with painted throats
Diving for fish swimming 'round and around
Like musical notes.

DEJÀ VU
(Quebec)

They do not exist, I know—this outdoor gallery of picturesque prints,
    this melancholy gossip of wind-song & salt,
These haunting fragments of laughter from shuttered courtyards
    winding down cobblestone side-streets,
This sonorous tincture of sunset regrets
    climbing like ivy-geraniums up wrought-iron balconies,
    inviting us back to a time that never was . . .

They do not exist; they never did—these sights & sounds,
    this feeling, almost prophetic—waiting, expectant;
This place we have never been before, that seems so familiar;
These words, like the meaning of a dream,
    unremembered on waking,
Written down in a hand unconcerned with its own movements;
The bustle of morning traffic tuning up like a brass ensemble, a trembling
    riff of jazz piano under the eaves, the tempo & hubbub of crosswalks
    syncopated to the beat of avenue & boulevard . . .

The energy of the sun stored up in the hidden tissues of the brain!
    reorganized into this seaway vista of ferryboats & canvas sails
    snapping in the wind below the ramparts
    where gulls glide over chimneys & copper rooftops—
Strollers with parasols waltz along the promenade
    overlooking the dockyard thronged with barges & tugs . . .
The ghostly hagiography of steeples & gargoyles & candle-lit niches;
    an illuminated manuscript under stained-glass
    lying in a slant shaft of light . . .
Aromas & smells from fish-market pavilions & sidewalk cafes
    wafted through open windows . . .
Pausing at doorways, under lamp-posts & quaint bookshop shingles,
    longing for a lost land of shadows . . .

Up ahead, around the corner, the music of harp-strings beckons
    toward a small park with pigeons & benches in the watery,
    dappled shade of sleepy sycamores,
And here, to the smiling delight of wide-eyed children
    & the sound of applause,
    a statue in bronze suddenly springs to life
As a mime & magician dazzle curious passersby and—voila!
    with a flick of the wrist—make the whole scene disappear . . .

DARWIN'S CIRCUS

In the runaway windows of my eyes
Rides apocalyptic spring!
And under the Big Top of the Sky
I see some incredible things—

Darwin's Circus of Life evolves
As the Merry-Go-Round of the World revolves;
A man in a monkey suit stands up
While a little brass band of buttercups

Mimics the Cartwheeling Sun.
Here, where we swing our arms and run,
He plays on his calliope
Till the animals rise from the sea!

In the Three Ring Circus of the Soul
Dandelions jump through a buttonhole,
In the center ring is a man on stilts—
The Fabulous Ego, taller than guilt—

Climbing out of a compact car.
Oh, it's really quite bizarre!
A backfire sounds, he starts to undress,
Down to a fig-leaf holiness;

And where he stood, a woman stands,
Holding a tree in the palm of her hand.

ANIMAL ALPHABETS

The alphabet of the alligator comes from an ancient aeon.
The biography of the Bear is a book about blackberries.
The chronicle of the Cicada is an underground classic.
The diary of the Dog is a dissertation on daydreams.
The encyclopedia of the Elephant is an epic of enormous eloquence.
In the fairytale of the Frog, the princess becomes a polliwog.
The grammar of the Grasshopper is a glossary of gamboling glyphs.
The Hippopotamus is sheer hyperbole; the Hummingbird, a hymn.
The itinerary of the Impala is an instance of *italics*.
The Jellyfish keeps its "Journal of the Medusa".
The Katydid gets its kicks quoting Keats off-key.
The Ladybug's lyrics are punctuated with polka-dots.
The Monkey's business is a metaphor for man.
The Nightingale's note is a numinous nocturne.
The Owl's "who" is the orphan's ode.
The parable of the Porcupine makes a poignant point.
"Quickly or quietly?" are questions for the Quail.
The Rhino is known for his ribaldry; the Raven, for raucous refrains.
The Spider's syntax is silkier than a sonnet by Shakespeare.
The Termite's terminology is the tree's tragic tale.
The Unicorn is an ungulate from an undiscovered universe.
The Vulture is well-versed in the vocabulary of veins.
The word-play of the Whale is written on the waves.
X is a signature in the eyes of extinct species.
The yap of the Yak is a yarn in Yakutsk.
The Zebra's zip-code is a zoo in Zimbabwe.

THE SPIRIT OF STALLIONS

A stallion is a spirit measured by hands
A panorama riding through a dream-catcher's hoop

Sounds becoming songs, the music of galloping time
A humming dynamo that becomes a haunting melody

It is a printed hoof curving into arabesques of calligraphy
The structure of a sentence yearning for an ornamental rhyme

A grace-note that comes by hard work & delicate touches
The nuance of light in a subtle frame

If the subject is beauty, it is the simplicity of friendship
Intentions beginning without pretense or complacency

Fleeter than sea-foam painted on the wind
Blind form endowed with the powers of omen

Surging in waves out of chaos, magic & divination
Drive & desire & instinct wilder than water

ARC OF THE MOON

arc of the moon, illumined:
a latticework of reveries,
a labyrinth of shadows;

the west wind, in delicate tendrils
pilots her island's triangular flocks
heaving her tropics in masses,

threading her purple surge, her barefoot escapes
finer than gossamer daydreams,
anemone staining the playthings of sunset.

Fecundity is her calendar of kelp, her ocean;
fairness is in her hand of flowering myrrh,
her sanctuary & sandy archipelago.

Albatross & turtle celebrate
her temple atoll, her sacred grove
arranged in the mind like a shoal—

micro-protozoa giving way
to wavelengths of aura & song—
the rapture of a dewdrop, collapsing . . .

Earth's hanging gardens
mapped out over a millennium
perfect her indiscretions.

Detritus of the moon:
a honeycomb, a horny spine,
a shipwrecked hull

where nautilus & nymph,
whorled in their urchin tentacles,
ply with dolphins in amorous intrigue.

COMPOST

My days are scrubbed away by rain;
My hours by hands as rough on stone
As scouring tides, till what remains
Is smoothed, removed, or rearranged.

Out of mulched leaf, dry heap of bone,
Of ash and rag, or peel and rind,
Of egg-shell shards and coffee grounds
The compost of my soul refined:

The rich turned earth atoned in what
The lowly worm has humbly but
Sublimely left behind: wet wings
Light-mingling with the roots of things.

Edward Fisher

CLOUD ATLAS

Clouds are a project of imagination superimposed over a dew-point;
Particles of dust & smoke & ocean-salts vanishing vertically in delicate
    wisps,
Sublimated droplets transitioning into visible vapors, limned at the
    limits . . .

Homer imagined the outline of Olympia like a sandy shore,
Dante caught glimpses of coming glory illuminated from within;
Shakespeare saw monumental citadels & towering promontories.

Clouds are a gentle reverie reflecting the mood of the dreamer—
Majestic summits on the move, like the mountains of the moon,
Festooned with feathered interstices iridescent in aspect . . .

The ancients fancied a chariot for Apollo, a cuckoo-land of dragons,
A twilight vision of Elysian fields suffused in a golden light,
A fleeting armada, an argosy of ghost-ships in search of an antique
    realm . . .

Clouds conceal a wing-woven other-worldliness formed in
    phenomenal waters;
Radiant halos & veils, celestial exaltations of Biblical origin—
A tabernacle, a countenance, a prophetic message, a throne . . .

Time passing in absent-minded self-absorption & unknowing solitude,
Layers of daylight arranged in featureless, windblown heaps;
Parallel thoughts in rippling waves, undulating out over shallow seas . . .

A cry of alas from earthlings, the echoing voice of departure & longing
Lost in the endless windows & pitiless indifference of a melancholy
    city skyline,
The rumpled bed-sheets of exiled lovers, poised in passionate poses . . .

Clouds are a symbol of mutability & the foolishness of men—
A metaphor for metamorphosis mocking our own mortal destiny;
Gloomy garlands of gathering wool, trophies to sorrow & loneliness

The intersection of roiling tempests brooding over immeasurable quiet,
Anvil-shaped masses of cumulonimbus hammered out by a barbaric
    sun
Mirror-silvering the hilltops, lofty, triumphal, in tumult!

Clouds are the thundering hoof-beats & horseheads of apocalypse
Swaggering over the deep—the haunting laughter of shadows
And the grumbling stomach of the gods, forever hungry to make
    history . . .

Edward Fisher

LORD OF THE MAGIC HAMMER
(Thursday)

I am the Lord of the Magic Hammer
Thundering bolts back, slamming shut doors;
Quarrelsome, boisterous, rain-god of terror,
Dark clouds at midnight, storms from the north!

Wandering thumbprint, cracked voice of havoc,
I am the grumbling curmudgeon of doom!
Hungry wolves howl in the sack of my stomach;
I know where the sun sleeps, the age of the moon.

Wind-eyed at blood-tide, whirling in circles,
Walking the morning at war with the world!
Axe-smite & sword-strike, ruins of castles—
Wake wrath & vengeance, rule at your will!

ARCADIAN GRACES

The forest is on fire in the fall!
Each trembling leaf is a tongue of flame
Consuming all the colors of sunlight
Stored up in the splendor of sugary veins—
A limned illumination of in-laid gold.

Listen to the stillness as your hands retrace
The broken characters of the heart
With jointed fingers disguised as twigs—
The phantom branches of the standing dead
In the migrating shapes of words . . .

And the sounds of the voice in parting
Flowing like a river out of the moon,
Blowing over tomorrow for the last time
As Io collects her secret vowels—
Ephemeral sections of woodwinds & strings . . .

An elegant arrangement of tiny cells
Flush with the edge of the four-cornered night
In a world that is always falling,
Mixing reflection with signs from the sky
In a deep intermingling design.

Edward Fisher

The instrument of the cascading rain
Transforming the morning star through a cross-pane,
Blurred by the tears of a child's bad dreams,
Obscuring a land unremembered on waking
Unveiling Arcadian graces.

Taproots of earth, season of shadows,
Speaking in spectrums of slow-motion sap,
Teach me the wisdom of each turning leaf—
Mystery of happiness, sweetness of life
Trapped in a narrowing network of change . . .

THE RESIDUE OF DAY

My life by sleep is halved away
Into an idle argument:
The dreamy residue of day.

From wind-blown clouds, sun-split by rays,
Aslant, a shaft of light descends
Through rainbow realms with gold in-lay

Bright tints of autumn on display,
The moon in curving increments,
All gathered up and swept away . . .

An oriental moth at play
Upon a candle-flame intent
Where Lao-Tzu has lost his way.

Explaining what I meant to say,
Gainsaying things I never meant;
Betrayed by silence, shades of gray.

My soul in secret, selved away;
My face and name and fingerprints,
All hues and hints of yesterday
Redeemed in dreams, erased by day.

LOOSE LEAF

Bone dry
blown by
an autumn wind
in slow-motion tumbling, end over end
downcast from the sky
back to earth again
last leaf in the land.

These falling leaves recall the fall of man
the falling world
reveals me as I am:
impossible to find
myself, in time
anymore.

Squirrels scurry
hurry home
with acorns in their mouths,
hope fills my hollow heart
bare limbs and empty head;
still as the standing dead,
holed up in worry.

Prayers cup the air!
held breaths let go
warm small hands and are gone
like sparrows flying south
each sigh distilled: a whispered ghost
a shadow on the ground.

The furnace and inferno of the sun,
the burning eye of heaven—
raging, ageless—
as seasons turn with sticks for arms
on blind men in the snow.

RAINSPOUTS ARE ALL ICY

Rainspouts are all icy,
Geese in flight
Depart with cold tradition;

Seeming to know
Which way to go,
Keep pace with teaching seasons.

On human tongues a tale of woe:
The windblown words "I know, I know"
Make peace with earth below.

Down from a sky like lead it comes!
As if the eye of heaven drew its lid
Close to the ground;

Flecks from the painted dome of day
Fill up the street.
Gone all the lovers' beds adrift—

Those whispered signatures that seemed
Unlike the others, aimless and unique,
Like angels in the snow . . .

A breathless ghost like zeros takes their place—
The winter in a sack, come back
Black-windowed from the north.

The long road withers to a distant dot
Like sentences to nowhere;
White rows of hooded figures come to town.

The Big Bear in the dark cave of the moon
With padded paws
Leaves footprints in the stars . . .

Edward Fisher

SOFT SNOW SLOW SINKING

soft snow
slow sinking
softer still
than great lace napkins
better still
than lilies dally
side-to-side
come settle on
my windowsill

through chimney soot
on cottage roofs
pine-tufted, circling
sheets of ice,
glass miniatures
of steeple towns
their earthbound churches
upside down
as carolers and lights
fill up the street

seems like the world
has fallen fast
into some starless realm
swept from some lost
forgotten past
white flakes adrift
slow-sifting still
drop into night's
dead-letterbox . . .

PERFECT SNOW

Nothing is given freely, nothing kept,
Except for this lone presence, these wild eyes
Devouring themselves in some ritual death
Tracked back to a circle of sacrifice.

The story: a quarrel of antlers beneath
Dark pines in the night, where the perfect snow
Piles up in drifts & the wind bares its teeth
Taking bites from the moon, at forty below.

Old Eskimo know the hunger of life,
Smearing raw flesh on a sharp, upright blade;
And, drawn to the scent of the whetted knife,
The wolf, at his own howling blood, tongues away . . .

Till the cave bear grumbles awake and yawns,
Till the terns wing home in the arctic spring,
Till the salmon return in the fall to spawn—
Forgiveness, eternal, in everything.

Edward Fisher

ABOVE THE TREE-LINE

If you look deep enough, you will see it;
If you listen long enough you will hear—
Beyond that distant range, life has its limits;
An unexpected precipice, a star
Calling your name everywhere you turn,
Echoing all over the curve of the earth!
At the desert's edge, the whispering thorn
Whistling indifferently, beckons you north.

Birds crying in a sky-blue vertigo
At the ocean's verge, a surface fin
Foretelling all—the inevitable O—
A fate apprehended, an inkling, a sense
Touring the contours of clouds all day;
That comfortable zone where your earthbound plans
Tug at your dreams, and gravity gives way
To human error, accident and chance.

Above the tree-line, on the windswept slope,
The landscape draws a blank across the mind;
No footprints go where stunted dwarf-pines grow
In snow and granite: nature's warning sign
Bordering on a realm of mists and lakes,
Haunting the stillness of a mirrored sky,
Inviting you into the black bear's domain
Of old growth trees, to teach you how to die.

ZYGOTE

Something drives me on,
Like salmon in season
Upstream to spawn, leaping
Turning white in white water . . .

Hurtling headlong toward fall
And all its changing colors;
Gone against rainbow grain,
Against all odds and on . . .

And so I go, ego struggling
Embryo to ear evolving
Zygote to polliwog wriggling
Sea-goat beginnings . . .

My engineered, amphibian brain
Marooned in a magical body;
A destiny, prehistory, or dream
Under the heavenly maps of the moon.

Thrust into new worlds bottoms up!
Breathless, ashore out of sleep . . .

THE DAYS GO DANCING ROUND THE POLES

At castle bridge and barbican
A bearded, two-faced god stands guard,
Deploying boisterous armies north
As ice-storms slam his iron gate;
The wind cries out, an orphan sound,
As hungry wolves come back to town.
Under an arching, single star,
Swing wide the bolted doors of war!
Warm days are but an old man's dream:
He rocks his chair and stokes the coals.
Like chimney smoke, his memories
Dance with the days around the poles.

This is the month the world began!
Its borrowed days still lengthen, and
Awakening on drowsy lids
With light regrets, renews its buds.
Young lovers blow a morning kiss,
Their foreheads wreathed in silhouettes,
While those homebound in wedded bliss
Wish they were free of vows instead.
Ring bells of angels! Storied bowers!
Uncertain glories in the flower!
Wet wings of butterflies unfold
As dancing days go round the poles.

With noisy robins on the lawn,
Propitious gods, baptismal fonts,
Bouquet of faces, dewy locks,
Prelude to beauty's music box—
All praise his name with food & drink,
Imperial fruit, majestic grain,
The spectacle of ancient kings,
The Sun in triumph rules and reigns!
Cast off your garments, mend your mood,
Let harvest brew and dregs take hold,
Nor spare the claret's blushing rude—
The dance of days around the poles.

A faded leaf faints with the year,
Its russet colors all distilled
On sunset walks, in hay-gold tincts,
From meadow moon to bobolink.
A dismal sky fills up with gray,
Stark widow-makers etch the earth;
Chill rain and melancholy mist
Forsake me in my changed estate.
My winter palace under siege,
Its frosty solstice in revolt,
Passed Saturn's throne and outer rings
The days go dancing round the poles.

LOVE'S COMPASS ROSE

SLEEP LAY LONG

sleep
lay long
  like
        wings
        masks
lips,
  let her
  and

palms
crossing

        eyes
        dividing

  her
        ,
  circular

        egg
        suggestion

  springs
    by her

        hold
          her
  and the mouth
    the inside

        was again
        hers

ROUGHLY, SOFTLY

Roughly, like the animal of sin,
My love comes in her naked mood, her beauty;

Wildfires spread like fingers on her skin
And leap up through her body!

Her kiss, blown like a leaf upon the wind,
Breath-taking as her blessedness is naughty . . .

But then, into a waterfall she turns,
And counter to her plunge, renews her rainbows:

She flows, flows like a river and returns
Softly now to me, embracing shadows;

The face of earth, the yearning moon full-term,
Become her sacred places, thumb and elbow.

THE LAND WHERE LOVE LIES DOWN

This is the land where love lies down;
We shall whisper a prayer and kiss the ground
And tread like a snail on a leaf.

Windy and wild how the heart flies home;
When her wing is mended, she will sing her song,
And eat from my palm like a dove.

Salty and bronzed now the hero returns;
He shall lay down his arms from war,
And wake with the dew in his beard.

This is the shore where the sea bows down
Among the golden grains of time
Washed by the waves, and built with children's hands.

WONDERFUL INDIGO TAPESTRY

Wonderful indigo tapestry
Woven of female and male

Beasts in a cloudy menagerie
Cherubs in whistling sails

Love is the flower of antiquity
Kept from the sea's old betrayal

Home like the dove from the enemy
Kisses that end fairytales

LAND OF THE LOST AND FOUND

Over one day to another
As the sun leaves behind
The shadow of trees
Like lovers, entwined,
And kisses shaped like leaves,
Flocks wing their way to sea.

I know that time can wear
The rough stone smooth,
And that the mind is skipping there
Across the waves,
In time perhaps,
Or in the heart eternally,
As love is possible
Only eternally.

Here at last, where the river ends
And the sun comes tumbling down,
From one lover's arms to another's
In the land of the lost and found:
Loves that will always be,
And anxiety
Quiet as the moon.

My life the light wind kisses
And carries to the hill
The star that, in its fall
Still misses
The other stars,
The other stars.

HEART OF DOVE & WING OF SPARROW

Heart of dove & wing of swallow
Heal this lover's open wound,
Conjure up a vanished shadow
Trace a circle on the ground.

Bone of sparrow, sacred entrails,
Take this naked pain away,
Lure with spells & sphere of crystal
Even Venus must obey.

Still the waves & tame the tempest,
Weave her tales of make believe;
Root of hare-bell, egg of red-breast,
Gathered in on St. John's Eve.

Artifice of sleepy eyelid
Make her dreams & secrets mine;
Pentacle, perfume of orchid,
Rapture unsurpassed in rhyme.

Prove this formula & potion,
Chart her star & horoscope;
Charm her heart, lay siege her passion,
Map her palm & compass rose.

Smoke of incense, magic candle,
Sign & seal of Solomon;
Fire of vervain, verse eternal,
Flesh & blood become One song.

WALK SOFTLY IN MY GARDEN

The shape of your mouth is wicked
But I can see your beauty in your feet;
Walk softly in my garden, love,
Whatever fruit you find there you may eat.

The moon in the night is naked;
The snake in the tree is hidden.

The snail of your tongue, light-treaded,
Comes whispering luxurious alarms!
The circle of your kiss, my love,
A falling planet ringed around by charms.

A dream of the sea, my ballad;
The sounds in a shell, your siren.

The curve of your brow & eyelid
Perfecting heaven's petalled, flowering song;
My heart waits night & day, my love,
Where desert nectars sleep & shadows long.

The ways of the world are crooked
Eavesdropping on earthly Edens.

THERE WERE BIRDS IN THE ROOM THIS MORNING

There were birds in the room this morning,
Leaves in your hair where you slept,
Where you fell

Whirled all around in the round world's windows,
Sprung from the mind like a gear
And winding toward shadow

Sound asleep on the pendulous earth,
On the dark forest floor of the night.

No printed rose on a cotton pillow,
Nor butterfly dream curled up like a cat,
But spun out of time and crazy with tears.

There's a bird on my nerves that's calling, calling:
Like some incredible seashell,
Some delicate, beautiful

Egg of a birth
Come face-to-face with the moon!

HUSHED HOSANNAS

Hushed hosannas through the hay gold prairies,
Groundhog shadows in February,
Bluff as stallions on the bareback hills—
These are her moods, untamed, unbroken.

Rainbow manes through a wreath of flowers,
Runaway skies into sudden showers,
Wild as the sea and the way sweat smells—
These, her arrivals, with nostrils swollen.

Heartbreak in waves, hoof-beats like pulses
Drummed in the blood, curvet to crisis;
Rough tongues licking my salted palms—
This, her farewell, once the apple's eaten.

Edward Fisher

WÏTH PÖETRY ÖN MY LÏPS
(for Gayle)

I awoke this morning with poetry
On my lips, out of a dream of new life,
Naked & free of idle encumbrances,
The guitar of my old songs broken to bits
And only the woman I love by my side;
Shed of the sea and all its remonstrances,
Shed of the night and its dream of the sea,
Shed of myself and all past remembrances . . .

Junk of Sargasso, seaweed & salt
Strummed on the haunting waters of dawn,
Awake among breakers, the strands of my songs
Shaped like the woman with shells in her hair;
Her island of shadows gathers its gulls,
Her melody curved like the moon to a Moor . . .

HELOÏSE & ABELARD

Who could wish to be anywhere else
But here, where we make our bed?
Our hearts, daring everything!
Our dreams, dancing with death . . .

Shy as traveling woodland deer
Nibbling on acorns & leaves,
Stark widow-makers litter the path
Where we leave our tracks . . .

Our joy destroys the spangled night!
Its richly-decked miraculous vault
Hung with ornamental planets
On a seamless pavement of stars . . .

A river is singing in my blood,
Coursing along my wrists & throat,
Rooted in all directions,
Encompassing a wounded world!

Eternity unwinds its adventures in time
As the center is rediscovered everywhere
In the nowhere circumference
Of your lips & mouth . . .

And here, once again, briefly glimpsed,
The raven nature of beauty
Numinous as a dewdrop
Asleep at my side . . .

And I am Tristan & you are Isolt
Or you are Heloise & I am Abelard
Forever with my little pail of ambrosia,
And you, with your hair full of rain.

PRESSED PETALS

Pressed petals in a book of psalms
   Not long outside the womb,
Love's faces, daydreams, feathered rests;
   This cloud that eggs me on—
Securely as a snail whose tongue
   Is selved in porcelain;
The sun that tugs the moon along
   And tucks the oceans in.

In dreams, before our child was blessed,
   Its gender yet unknown,
I saw you hold a tender breast
   And draw a small head down.
Among wet wings and leafy lids,
   Shy brow and drowsy eye
I heard the birds cry out for joy:
   "Mother-of-pearl for girl or boy!"

And so the sky was all a-tilt
   And built like kingdoms come,
That day the Milky Way was spilt
   In circles round her thumb;
Some coconut dropped from my palms,
   A sea-whorl in her hair;
At hand, the whispered names of God
   Are cupped and cradled there.

LOVE SONG

If you were a flower of the earth
I would be a fumbling bumble-bee
Scaling your petals of nectar

If you were a firefly in the meadow
I would be its dance at evening
Pulsing through glowing scripture

If you were a blue sky at sunset
I would be a cloud of silver shadows
Tinged with burgundy & amber

If you were a map of heaven
I would be your compass rose
And the seven directions of the heart

If you were the night woods full of snow
I would be the lullaby of the moon
Etched over antlers & branches

If you were the distance between the stars
I would be the hands of the clock
Ticking slowly toward forever

If you were water for tea & spices
Let the cup that holds you
And warms your lips be me

If you were an inkwell
I would be the tip of the feathered quill
That writes this down

Let the passion of our hearts unfolding
Be like the fragrance of the strawberry
Succulent & ripe & sweet

Let the strength of our bond & embrace
Echo like the melody of songbirds
Returning in the spring

COORDINATES

In my imagination, east
And west are one, they meet;
Between them none, of each the least
Divided at my feet.

In my imagination, light
And darkness all the same:
Dews drink up day, dreams drop by night
And both go by my name.

In my imagination, left
And right are fused—one brain!
My muses introduced bereft
Of half-moon, cleft, or twain.

In my imagination, doubt
And faith co-equal sums;
The heart with all its stops pulled out—
The breath of earth all mum.

In my imagination, man
And woman counterpoised,
Stand in the garden, hand-in-hand:
One source, one house, one voice.

TIME'S VOICES SPEAK THROUGH ME

Time's voices speak through me, they are of old,
Repeating leaves bespangled with shaped hours
And, as the rainbow's anchored, so her gold,
Is carried off in pails by sails and flowers;
Intrigue of cobwebs, dust of star debris,
Delicate wings arising from cocoons,
The sea that is withdrawing to the sea,
Spilt milk below the belly of the moon.

Who seeks my castles, going up for sale,
Washed by the waves and built with children's hands?
Once heir to airy yonder, fairytales
Beyond a yawn or, in a wink, lost lands . . .
Time's sordid gesture kept in time's repose;
Love's earthly secret, shut up like a rose!

Edward Fisher

O, THE PERFECT POETIC

O is the perfect poetic
To symbolize the moon;
O is aught, a separate music,
Sigh's circumference and zone.

O is zero, heaven's cipher
With a snake's tale in its mouth;
O is all when life is over
And forgotten in the earth.

Voice or vowel, a horn of plenty,
Acorn store for yawning squirrels;
Shape of O—a hollow, hungry
Feeling waiting to be filled.

Almost holy, like a halo,
Blessed morning in the midst;
Nested note a-rush with swallows,
Plucked fore-flower of a kiss.

Knot of words, breath in the taking,
Pains to pearl the oyster's ache,
At the awful end of brooding
Standing upright like an egg.

82

ABOUT THE AUTHOR

Edward Fisher was born in Ohio & spent his boyhood as a military brat, touring castles on the Rhine & strolling down the Champs Elysees. As a teenager in the 60s, he watched tanks roll through the Heart of Dixie on their way to Ole Miss & rode out an earthquake in Alaska. After graduating with a bachelors in Literature from Reed College in Portland, Oregon, he joined the Peace Corps, surviving his tour of service in Uganda in the aftermath of Idi Amin's bloody coup. He holds a doctorate in psychology & worked with special needs children as a play therapist & adventure-based counselor. He is currently living with his wife in the foothills of the Catskills in upstate New York. His first book of poems is titled *Conversation with a Skeleton.*